THE HOMELY BEAR

by Daniel Kantak

Parson's Porch Books

The Homely Bear
ISBN: Softcover 978-1-960326-99-7
Copyright © 2024 by Daniel Kantak

Parson's Porch Books is an imprint of Parson's Porch *&* Company (PP*&*C) in Cleveland, Tennessee. PP*&*C is a self-funded charity which earns money by publishing books of noted authors, representing all genres. Its face and voice is **David Russell Tullock** (dtullock@parsonsporch.com).

Parson's Porch *&* Company *turns books into bread & milk* by sharing its profits with the poor.

www.parsonsporch.com

THE HOMELY BEAR

To all homely bears...
for their wisdom,
for their truth,
for their beauty.

The Homely Bear

She was a homely bear
whose coat was black,
whose coarse fur had
a gnarly nap.

She roamed the forest
and climbed its trees.
She slept in caves
so she would not freeze.

She had a stub tail
that would not wag.
In her left ear
she wore a game tag.

One day Bear
was down in the dumps
searching through trash
for edible lumps,
when out of the gulls
who swirled overhead
one gull flew down,
landed and said,

13

"Tell me Bear,
is what I heard true?
They say at the sand bar
that the top bear
is you."

Bear looked up
without emotion
and asked,
"Why are you here
so far from the ocean?"

"Bear, I'm the daughter
of the Master Bird.
I inherit his nest
when he gives the word."

"But wearing the sea star
here on my breast
won't make me a queen
when I sit on his nest."

21

"There are things
of the sea,
things of the land,
so many, many things
that I don't understand."

Bear put a paw
under her chin,
she spoke softly
with a wide grin,

"You gave up the sea,
the sand, the tide,
you gave it up
to be by my side?

Little bird,
do you know what I am?
I'm princess of nothing.
I'm queen of a sham.
I am hunted by that
creature called Man."

Gull flew up
and stood
on Bear's head,
and from that perch
she stopped Bear
and said,

"You're kind
and you're gentle.
You're brave
and you're wise.
You tell the truth
and don't live with lies.

I have sought you out
to be in your reach.
A fledgling I am
to the lessons you teach."

29

Bear smiled and said,

"Then stay if you will,
my feathered friend.
Keep dawn in your heart
until journey's end."

"Let the stars
be our blanket,
the forest
our road.

Let the
language of love
be our
 unbreakable code."

33

The end,
of the beginning.